Moving To Spain
"From Dream To Reality"

The Living In Spain Series
Book 1

By David Wright

CONTENTS

Chapter 1   Why Spain

Chapter 2   The Dream

Chapter 3   Research Saves Time And Money

Chapter 4   Papers You Will Need When Moving To Spain

Chapter 5   Rent Or Buy

Chapter 6   Moving Day

Chapter 7   The Fastest Way To Learn Spanish

Chapter 8   Finding Work In Spain, how and where

Chapter 9   Running A Business In Spain

Chapter 10   Your Kids In Spain

Chapter 11   Making Spanish Friends

Chapter 12   Traveling Around Spain

Chapter 13   Life in Spain after Brexit

INTRODUCTION.

This book was written to help others who are thinking of **moving to Spain**.

All info is based on my personal experiences and views, the information could be subject to change at any time and although I try to keep the information here updated things are changing with Brexit fast and you should always get professional legal help when moving to Spain.

Each year more and more people are thinking of moving to sunny Spain in search of a better way of life. For them and their family but there are many things you need to do and think about even before you consider a move to Spain and there is so much information to research. So now for the first time it's all right here in one place to access as and when you need it.

Many people Dream of living the dream life in sunny Spain but it can be a nightmare for those who don't get all the right information and do the proper research first. Be one of the people that gets it right the first time and learn here from people who have been there and done that and got the T shirt.

"If you want what others have,

you need to do what others do"

David has lived and worked in Spain for other people and companies as well as being self employed and running his own building and carpentry business here and over the years has employed all nationalities.

When first here David worked mostly for British expats here refurbishing their properties and this included bars and restaurants. He has seen many people come and go over the years some making it and others not, see why some succeed here in Spain and what they did, see the difference between those who failed here and learn buy mistakes David and they made so as your transition will be a smooth and successful one.

At the bottom of each chapter We have included reference links to info that David has used personally or has been recommended to him by friends here.

About the Author.

David Charles Wright,

is an English man, born in 1962, who became frustrated and disillusioned with the rat race 9 to 5 way of life and poor weather in the UK, so 18 years ago followed his dream and made the move to sunny Spain in search of a better way of life.

Going through a divorce and a global crisis that hit Spain hard, David has survived both and now married to Llani a Spanish girl for over 9 years he has extensive knowledge and contacts from both sides, English and Spanish, first as a British expat and from a Spanish resident with a Spanish wife and large Spanish family.

David has traveled all over Spain with his Spanish wife and to more than 20 other countries around the world including recently his dream destination of Bora Bora and Tahiti in the south Pacific and they still travel regularly, David has now stopped working on his own building business and bought a plot of land in Spain where he is working on his next major project of building his dream 4 bedroom villa here Almeria in Spain.

David has built up a very useful list of contacts all over Spain from trades professionals and estate agents all the way up to being personal friends with the British consulate here in Almeria.

David has appeared as an expert guest on the popular TV program."A Place in the Sun" David has done radio interviews for Costa del sol radio now on pod casts on Apple and spotify and this year been interviewed on the BBC news channel and featured in local magazines.

You can now get access to all his contacts and see the links to these here in his books.

Check out Davids Living in Spain Podcast show here

https://www.spreaker.com/show/living-in-spain-with-david-wright

Chapter 1
Why Spain

Each year thousands of British people up sticks and make the move to sunny Spain and for each one that does make that move there five more thinking and dreaming about doing it.

Spain's year round warm sun shine, mild winters and healthy diet along with a more laid back out doors lifestyle is very appealing to people fed up with the long cold UK winters, Unpredictable summers and the 9 to 5 rat race the UK has brainwashed many into following.

It's not just the weather though, Spain has many very different regions from white sandy holiday beaches to the snowcapped mountains and lust green valley's with sleepy time forgotten villages. There really is something for all tastes here and in just a few hours' drive you can change from one to the other.

Latest surveys have now put Spain at the top of the list and shown that people do live longer in Spain, Maybe it's the weather, the diet or just the way of life here but whatever it is, Spain has become the number one place British people are moving to and being just a few hours plane ride away its sort of a no brainer.

What do you want? Long quiet sandy beaches, snowy mountains and hillsides or the orange and olive tree covered country side? It's all here in One place.

The rich history and colorful culture of Spain and the people along with the many local fiestas that are almost a weekly occurrence here, makes life here interesting and entertaining for all the family all year round not just the summer months.

Personally my life here is very different now and not just because I am married to a Spanish girl. I am outdoors way more than when I lived in the UK and Enjoy more things out doors as the days are longer and warmer here. You don't have to worry that much about whether it will be nice at the weekend to have say a BBQ, it's always nice here. well mostly always.

It's all about the quality of life here. When you get up in the mornings and you open the curtains and see its sunny again it just make you feel good. OK weather is not everything but it does help. Wearing lighter thinner cloths is more comfortable than heavy jumpers and coats.

Safety In Spain

Yes there are parts of Spain that have crime like anywhere but here in Spain I see very few fights or drunkenness. I guess that's down to the fact that you can get alcohol here just about anywhere and at any time, so people don't binge drink like in the UK.

In the 17 years that I have been here I can honestly say that I have only seen about 4 drunk people in the streets and I am afraid to say they were all Brits on holiday here.

Spain is Safe for all the family and a great place to educate and bring up kids. It may be very different than the UK but it's all just a few hours away waiting to be explored.

CHAPTER 2
THE DREAM.

First off let me say that dreams do come true and you really can do anything you want, if you really want it enough, even if it seems impossible at first but most dreams fail to even get off the mark because people think they can't really have it. Plus a dream without action is just a dream, it takes hard work and daily action to make any dream a reality.

There is always a way to get what you want in life if you just look for it hard enough and find the right people to follow. Like the saying goes..

"if you want what others have got, then you need to follow and do what others are doing"

So your dream is to move to sunny Spain right? Well what are you doing about it?

Have you even been there yet? Spain is a big country and differs from the north to the south and has very different climates. Have you made lists of where you like and what you need, papers you have to fill in? There is so much you can do even before you move to Spain that can really help make your move there a smooth one and give you a head start above most others and these things cost little to nothing to start with. I will show you below.

Research Is Everything.

Research is easy now with the internet, all you need to do is type in a few places to start getting an idea of where you may wish to live and as you do start searching you will come across things of interest that will help you to refine your search to pin point the right place for you.

The more you start to research about **moving to Spain** the more you will find out and come across new things you may not have thought about that you need as you are searching.

Today the online world is a great way to get all the information you may need fast and it's just sifting through what's right for your needs.

There are some great [Facebook groups](#) that are full of expats that are living in Spain and can help with any questions you may have.

Here's a great one to start with [British Expats In Spain](#) facebook group "www.facebook.com/groups/BritishExpatsInSpain"

Most People want to *move to Spain* for the weather and the way of life, as Spain has year round warm sun shine and the healthiest diet in the world.

People really do live longer lives in Spain it's a fact and this is not just down to the diet of fresh fruit, fish and veggies but the slower pace of life and the more outdoors style of life you live here. Yes the weather is great here and this has a lot to do with the better life here, as you will find that you are more active here as the weather is good you are more out and about enjoying life rather than sitting in doors watching repeats on TV.

I remember just a few days ago I called my brother who lives in Brighton in the Uk as I was sitting on the beach at 4pm having a cold beer with a group of my Spanish friends.

He was watching TV with the heating on and the curtains drawn as it was getting dark there, Just 2 hours away by plane and such a different life.

There are many reasons why you may not be able to **move to Spain** or think you can't do it yet but these arc your own personal excuses. Brits living in Spain have all been through the same things and found a way to do it and so can you.

 If it's your dream then you owe it to yourself and your family to make it work.

Life is short, so get busy living now.

What's better.?.. reaching 85 years old sitting in the nursing home saying.....

 "i wish i had done that" Or Sitting on the beach in the sun saying **"I am so glad I did this".**

Years ago when I first started work in the UK I worked as a cabinet maker for a small family firm and there was an old guy there that trained the new boys. His name was Jim and he always went on about how in just 8 months he would be retired and out playing golf all day thinking of us young lads working hard. All a bit of a joke really but this went on right up until he did retire.

His last day the boss let him finish 10 mins early so we could say good bye and they gave him a watch.

4 weeks later our boss told us that Jim had died in his sleep that night.

All his life working hard for a watch and 4 weeks off and a pension he never got to enjoy.

I knew then that there had to be a better way.

Don't let life pass you by.

If it really is your dream to **move to Spain** then you and only you can make it happen.

How much do you want it and what are you doing now to start making it happen?

Join our free online group and get first hand tips from other expats..<u>British Expats In Spain</u>

Chapter 3
Your Research will save you time and money

Start looking at different places you may like to live in Spain like beach, hills small village or big city, inland or coastal areas they are very different and although you may think you would like to live in the country, what about winters there and how will you get to the doctors if you are ill there.

If it's the beach life you seek that's great but in the summer months it can get very busy and parking a nightmare. Plus can you really take it when it gets over 100 here for weeks at a time as it does each year in the summer months, it's nice for a week's holiday but living here long term is quite different. Maybe something in between.

Start making lists.

Open a file on your pc or write it down on paper and start thinking of what you now think you may need and then research it and file it for later. There is a load of info out there and you can adjust what you find and narrow it down to what you think is relevant to you and your needs.

Years ago back in the UK I went to hotel presentations where they were promoting Spanish property and this is a great way to see what you can get for your money and all the different areas but remember that each show normally pushes one area of Spain that they are promoting but if you go to several over time you get to see the bigger picture.

Inspection flights sound great and the thought of a cheap holiday to see the property may sound like a great idea but these promoters will hound you all day trying to get you to commit to a deposit so they can get their commission and can end up being a weekend nightmare.

Best way is to book a cheap short recon trip. Not a holiday though. Go to the area you think you like just to go looking at property, schools and chat with expats that live there to see how they live and what it's really like.

OK have a few beers sure but don't waste time sitting on the beach sun bathing, You can do that all day when you live there, this is a recon trip to get info and facts.

Go to a few estate agents and ask if they can take you to see property that's in your budget as this is a great way to see the area and what you can get for your money, plus the agent will tell you more info on the area so ask away as much as you can it's all free info that they will want to tell you, plus if it works out its where you want to buy you will have made a great contact for future trips.

If you do see a place or area you like then go back there later that evening or afternoon to see if the street is full of cars or screaming kids kicking a football against the cars. I had a client here several years back who bought a house here he had been to see 3 times with the agent and always in the mornings and when they moved in a few months later, the first day at 2.30pm there was a school at the end of his road and each and every day parents would pull up and double park right outside his house waiting to pick up the kids.

Hundreds of shouting kids would fill the street for about 30 mins and this was every week day for ever.

Handy if you have kids but could be a nightmare if you want a quiet life.

Online search.

The internet is great to do searches and has loads of info that can really help but if your Spanish is poor the chances are that you are searching online in English. There are great Spanish sites that you can still access and prices are often lower in Spanish.

If you were living in China and searched online for a car in china on an English site you would get way different results than if you searched online in Chinese or a Chinese site.

The same here in Spain.

Just a few months ago I was in the market for a new trailer for my car and I wanted a large

4 wheeled trailer to carry materials around in. I typed in the word for trailer in Spanish and searched local Spanish websites and got loads of local results and some great prices rather than the main dealers far away if I was searching an English site.

If your Spanish is not that great just Google the words and copy and paste them in the search, you will be shocked at the difference in results I think.

ONLINE SPANISH PAPERS.

You can now get access to Spanish news papers online and although you may not understand them that well you can see photos of property and prices to get a feel of costs and what's available in that area.

WHAT I DID.

once we made up our mind we wanted to move here my then wife and I booked a week in a cheap hotel here and went to the local British bars in the area to chat to the locals to get info.

The barmen here are the best source of info as they normally know everyone and all their business. You will find that the local expats love chatting about the area and that they know all the best places to go and where is a good area and what's not so good.

Also there is normally a British club of some sorts in most British areas that meet up once a week to chat and this is a great place to get info.

I found my first job in Spain this way and a cheap apartment to rent all from having a few drinks with the local Brits but don't get to drunk remember is a recon trip not a booze cruise.

Keeping all the info together in a list or file is great for later trips or questions about things you may want to ask others. Copy and paste things from your pc straight to a word doc to access later, this can be very helpful unless you have a perfect memory.

Some great online sites and search help about Spain.

https://www.milanuncios.com/inmobiliaria/

https://britishexpatsinspain.com/

https://wikitravel.org/en/Spain

https://goo.gl/TPrb6E

Chapter 4

IMPORTANT PAPERS YOU WILL NEED
Post Brexit.

There are many papers that you will need to have to stay in Spain and you will need many copies of all your details as Spain just loves paper work and its one of my pet hates here the fact that there is just so much of it.

So below are the main papers that you need when you first move to Spain.

British nationals who plan on living in Spain for more than 3 months must register as a resident and on the padrón at their town hall.

You should register in person at the "Oficina de Extranieros" (immigration office) in the province where you live or at the designated Police station

You will be required to provide your documents to support your application.

Important New Requirements post Brexit

The new law which sets out British citizens rights to register as residents under the Withdrawal Agreement, states that economic stability needs to be proven as per the law 240/2007 relating to EU citizens who wish to gain residency in Spain. This law states that each applicant should have (*recursos suficientes para no convertirse en una carga para la asistencia social en España durante su período de residencia*) "sufficient resources not to become a burden for social assistance in Spain during his period of residence".

Unfortunately, it doesn't state the exact paperwork that is required to prove this.

How is "proof of economic stability" calculated?

In Malaga, as with many other regions the income requirements are based on a system called IPREM which stands for "The Public Multiple Effects Income Indicator" which is what the Spanish Government uses to calculate the **minimum** income requirement and is a base for the Benefits' system in Spain.

Currently (2021), IPREM is:

- IPREM Mensual: €564.90 (monthly minimum income)
- IPREM Anual: – 12 pagas: €6,778.80 (annual minimum income, paid in 12 payments)

This is probably what all the comments and threads saying "I've been told I need €7k in a bank account in Spain" are based on.

So how do you prove "Economic Stability" to the Immigration Office
You need to prove you have either income or savings (or both) so let's start with income.

Post Brexit you now need to show 30,000 in a bank in UK or Spain and have a private

health insurance paid in full for at least 1 year.
You must now apply in the country of your birth.

If you are married or have a legal partner then the second person needs to show proof of 7,000 so that means a married couple would need to show around 37,000 as funds before they can even apply.

These amounts may vary a little in different areas but they are a lot more than before Brexit so get processional help and advice before you even start the process.

Visas
There are now several new visas that you can apply for if you wish to stay longer than the 90 days in every 180 day rule.
To be certain what visa is right for your needs you need to get processional help and advice.

The Spanish authorities will issue you with a credit-card-sized residence certificate, probably now you will get the new TIE card for the first 5 years that's renewable to permeant, if you have been living in Spain for 5 years or more then you will get the 10 year TIE card.

What they will ask for...

Do you have a salaried position or you are self-employed in Spain

- ☐ or you can support yourself and your family, and you have a public or private health insurance that provides full cover in Spain
- ☐ or you are a registered student at an educational establishment recognized by the Spanish authorities, and you can support

yourself and have a public or private health insurance with full cover in Spain

- [ ] or you are a family member of an EU national that meets one of the previous conditions. The family member can be:
- [ ] If in the case of a student: his/her spouse or common-law partner, or his/her children
- [ ] In other cases: his/her spouse or common-lay partnr, his/her children or spouse´s children up to 21 years old or incapable or his/her ancestors.

In all of these cases, you must still register with the Central Register of Foreign Nationals (**Registro Central de Extranjeros**), no later than **3 months** after arriving in Spain.

What you need to take With You

- [ ] Passport or other identity document (not expired)
- [ ] Official form (EX-18), two copies, filled and signed by the UE national.

In addition, you will have to attach other documents, depending on your situation:

- **salaried workers** – your contract of employment or other proof of your employment status. This also depends on what area you do it all in as many have different rules now.

- **self-employed workers** – proof of registration in the register of economic activities (censo de activities economics) or other proof of your employment status.

  not in employment in Spain? Proof of:
  (i) health cover valid in Spain and
  (ii) sufficient means to support yourself and your family.

- **Pensioners** – provide proof of public health cover.

Different offices ask for different things and not always the same requirements

Your N.I.E.

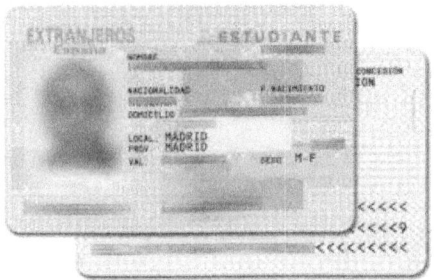

An NIE, is an abbreviation for Número de Identidad de Extranjero, which translates as Identification Number for Foreigners, or Foreigners' Identification Number if you prefer.

The NIE is your all-purpose identification and tax number in Spain. You need it for every official process in Spain. For example, you will need an NIE number to buy a property, buy a car, get connected to the utilities and most importantly as far as the Spanish state is concerned, pay your taxes.

Without an NIE number, the Spanish tax authorities are unable to assess or process annual tax payments such as income tax (IRPF), and the annual wealth tax (Patrimonio), both of which are declared by resident and non-resident property owners.

NIE numbers, in mid-2016 the regulation was changed to eliminate the three-month expiry deadline, so NIE numbers are now valid indefinitely. But this is Spain and the bureaucracy is a bit of a mess, and regulations are not uniformly implemented or even understood.

You may find that some notaries refuse to accept a certificate that is older than three months, which could cause problems for property buyers trying to sign deeds more than three months after obtaining their NIE certificate. In principle you can get your NIE number anytime before you buy, but to be on the safe side you might want to sort out your NIE number on your last trip to Spain, when you find a property you want to buy and can complete within three months.

Who needs an NIE in Spain?

1. Any foreigner who becomes resident for tax purposes in Spain needs an NIE number in Spain.

2. Any non-resident foreigner who buys property in Spain. If a couple buys a property in Spain together, and they register the property in both their names, then both of them must obtain an NIE number in Spain.

3. Anyone who wants to work in Spain, or start a business in Spain.

When do you need to have an NIE number?

If you are buying property in Spain, then you need to have an NIE number by the time you sign the deeds of purchase before notary, an event known in Spanish as the escritura.

Getting your NIE number in time for escritura means applying at least 1 month before hand if you are applying in Spain, and at least 2 months before hand if you are applying via a consulate abroad.

The actual time it takes depends upon where you apply, and the time of the year. You might be able to get an NIE number in person in Spain in a couple of days, but it could also take weeks, so best allow yourself plenty of time.

How do you apply for an NIE number?

The first thing to understand is that dealing with the Spanish bureaucracy is often a perplexing, not to mention frustrating affair. The way they interpret the regulations in

Andalusia might differ from the way they interpret the same rules in Catalonia.

In one area, for example Barcelona, you need to book an appointment online in advance to request your NIE number, then spend hours waiting in a queue, whilst in other areas you can just turn up and get everything done in half an hour. I have confirmed for myself that the rules are inconsistently applied, which makes it difficult to prepare a guide to NIE numbers.

So keeping in mind that the process and interpretation of requirements might be different depending on how and where you apply for an NIE number, here is a general guide that explains the official requirements and the process as it should work (but might not)

There are three ways to apply for a Spanish NIE number:

1. Apply in person in Spain.

2. Apply in person via a Spanish Consulate abroad.

3. Apply through a representative in Spain

Prepare the necessary documentation:

All applicants: Two copies of the Ex-15 application form filled out and signed . The Spanish name for the NIE form is Solicitud de Número de Identidad de Extranjero (NIE) y Certificados (EX-15),

All applicants: An original document (plus a photocopy) that justifies your reason for applying for an NIE number, such as a private purchase contract for a property, deposit contract, or a mortgage approval.

EU nationals: Your passport and a photocopy of the main page of your passport (the page that includes your photo, name, passport number, address, etc.).

Non-EU nationals: Your passport and a photocopy of your entire passport (all pages), plus proof of your legal entry into Spain (for instance a landing card, known in Spanish as a declaración de entrada or a título de viaje or cédula de inscripción). Some Oficinas de Extranjeros might accept a valid entry stamp in your passport as proof of legal entry.

 To be on the safe side non-EU nationals might also want to take along two recent passport size colour photographs with a plain colored background.

The new T.I.E. Card

(TIE, or *Tarjeta de Identidad de Extranjero*)

What is the TIE, exactly?

The TIE is a biometric card that contains the identity details of a foreigner who lives in Spain. For many years this has been the identity card for residents from outside the EU and the EEA. This card will now be issued also for British nationals with a special note stating that the holder benefits from the Withdrawal Agreement for residency purposes. This means that any British national who obtains the TIE before the end of 2020 will be able to carry on living in Spain from 2021 onwards with the same rights as before. The TIE will have the same validity as the green A4 paper document or card issued up until now.

Do I have to change my Green Card for the TIE?

Not necessarily. Both the new TIE and the EU Residency Certificate are equally valid as a residency document and will allow British nationals to benefit from the Withdrawal Agreement and secure their rights from 2021 onwards.

After five years residence registration you are entitled to apply for a certificate of permanent residence in Spain.

Changes to the residency regulations

Great tip here.

My ex accountant is now the chief British consulate in Almeria and he has people all over the country that can put you in touch with the right person to help you.

He is a friend of mine now and just ask for Alejandro and say David sent you, his

website is here..
http://gestoriasalvador.com/en/consulado-honorario-britanico/

There is a lot of papers to fill in and sort out when **moving to Spain** and even if you speak very good Spanish it is difficult and stressful so just pay people to do it for you but make sure they are the right people and always get a recommendation first.

There is now a smaller Residence card that you can get rather than the large A4 paper one, ask when you go to get yours as the small credit card size is easier to carry around.

The new tie card even better.

CHAPTER 5
RENT OR BUY

It's great to be able to buy a new *home in Spain* and even better if you have no mortgage but there are risks with buying and having **no mortgage** and advantages of renting first that could save you thousands.

Why I think renting first is best.

When I first came here I rented for 8 months and the 2 bed apartment was great, near the beach and easy to get to and from my then works.

The first few weeks we loved the apartment and thought it was all we ever needed and the location was perfect. Then the summer months came and our apartment backed onto the back of a hotel that had been quiet for weeks but now had started to get busy with tourists, so the kitchens were open at first light and now it was getting warmer they had all the kitchen windows open so we would be woken up at about 6 am to the sound of dishes being washed and thrown around getting ready for the morning breakfast rush.

This started to get a bit much every day and was later a reason why we did not want to buy in that area even though at first we loved it there. If we had bought there we would not have known this until months after we had bought.

Also renting first in an apartment or house you will see the daily routine of your neighbors that may or may not become a problem... like does the guy next door go to work each day on his old motor bike that he revs up each morning at 7 am. This is what a friend of mine has now every week day.

Only rent for 3 to 6 months as you can always ask for longer if you like it there and if you are paying on time the owners will want to keep you in there. You can also ask for small things when renting that the owner may try to get you to keep you happy there as the Spanish like long easy lets to Brits who pay on time.

 If you are renting longer then after 6 months you could ask for a rent reduction saying that you like it there but have found a cheaper place down the road. A friend of mine did this and got 50 euro's a month knocked off as he signed for another 6 months.

Renting a few months in different areas is a great way to see places before committing to buying a place .

Deposits.

Most agents will ask for 1 months deposited and 1 month up front this is the norm here now but I hear some people ask for 6 months up front and this is something that I would not recommend as I will explain later.

Normally going through an estate agent is best and they will get you to sign all the papers in their office, so if your Spanish is poor please take someone with you to make sure you really understand what you are signing for.

BIG TIP.

Most Spanish owners will try and get out of returning your deposit here.

I had this happen to me and have heard it here many times.

After 8 months of renting I asked the agent to come and see our apartment the day we moved out to see that it was clean and tidy with no damage. He didn't want to do this saying that it was not necessary but I insisted and he came.

Just 2 days later we went to the agents office to collect or deposit. He told us that the owner had to get in cleaners as it was so dirty and the cost was exactly the same amount as our deposit.

After protesting to him and him saying they had the right we just chalked it down to experience, so be warned. Many renters now stop paying one month before they leave to cover their deposits but you could get the agent and the owners to go to the rental and sign there and then saying it's all good.

Buying In Spain.

First off here check out my youtube channel as there are loads of videos I have

made with some really helpful that will save you money

https://www.youtube.com/c/DavidWrightBritishExpatsInSpain

When we were ready to buy our first place here in Spain we went to the bank to arrange the funds and transfer on a property we had seen that we had liked very much.

I asked to see the bank manager and to my surprise we knew him as he was living in the same apartment building we had rented and we said hi many mornings as we pasted in the hallway.

He sat us down and asked why we would not be having a mortgage on the property so I told him that we didn't need one as it was a 2 bed apartment and we wanted to have no payments to worry about.

This is what he told me...

You should get a mortgage even a small one as this means that the bank will do more searches on the property as they need to protect their investment and that way you will know that all the papers are ok and in order.

If we paid cash then the bank had no real interest and would not do the same amount of checks and we could be at risk.

We ended up having a mortgage of 10,000 euro's over 5 years that we could pay off at any time, this was a great way of getting it with less risk as I now know that there are so many illegal builds here or owners with papers that are out of date or incorrect.

I have just bought a plot of land here to build my new dream house and when we were looking we found an old house on the perfect plot and wanted to buy it to knock down the house to build our new house.

The price was right, the place was right and the agent and the owner told us that all papers were in order.

We have learned a lot here in the last 17 years so my now Spanish wife and I went to the local planning office to ask about the plot and the house on it. This you can do for free it's your right but most people don't know or don't bother.

The guy in the planning office found this old large book with all the buildings in that street and told us that the owner had never asked for the extension on the back so the building was illegal.

We told him that I wanted to take it down and build a new house so no problems right? no as the owner had not asked for permission for the small extension that would have cost about 3,000 euro's there would now be a fine of up to 20.000 or they would have to take it down before they could sell the house to us.

Nightmare or what....

We told the owner this and they said it would be fine as they would apply for the permission at the notary when we sign. The agent also said it would be ok but remember they just want their commission on the sale and get part of it if we put down a deposit.

My solicitor told me that this was **not** the case and that the planning office would probably not grant this now as they are cracking down on this sort of thing here.

Yes we pulled out of this one and later found a better place.

This goes on a lot here so if you don't want to go do your own checks or your Spanish is poor, then pay someone as it could save you big problems in the future and this is why you hear so many sad Brit stories here, they just don't do the checks.

When I went to buy my first house here about 10 years ago I found this new 4 bed house that had just been finished that was in a street of 5 houses all the same, all for sale but the 2 at the end of the road interested me so we went to see the first one and the Spanish agent told me on the phone that the price was 200.000 Euros.

The day I went to see it was with another agent but from the same office. who told me that the price was now 220,000. it has gone up 20,000 over night. So I went to the house next door that was the same but asking price 200,000 I spoke to the agent and we put down a deposit.

Just 2 days later the first agent called again saying that I could now have his house for the same 200,000 now. They do try it on here especially if you are English and can't speak Spanish.

Over the 18 years here I have bought and sold several properties and this is what you may have to deal with.

Buying land is a lot different than buying property and if you need a mortgage to buy land banks are not lending as much as for a house, as the land is harder for them to sell but once you have had designs passed and got the building permissions in place they will lend you more.

Getting a mortgage you should always shop around and even now I change my mortgage every few years to get the best deal. This may seem a lot of work but if you have a mortgage and you pay on time and you have all your direct debits and bills coming out of that one bank , they like to keep you or have you as a new customer so it's sometimes worth changing the lot to get the best deal and this is what we just did to buy our plot of land here.

Links and places on how and where to buy property. Also my contact at the British Consulate.

https://goo.gl/Sqa8LW

https://goo.gl/5js6yG

https://goo.gl/uWseVP

http://gestoriasalvador.com/en/consulado-honorario-britanico/

Chapter 6
Moving Day

Its finally here, the day you move. so are you going by car boat or plane and have you packed the kitchen sink?

By car.

Many Brits choose to take their UK car to Spain and although this can be the cheaper option it could end up costing you a lot more as well as being a real nightmare with paperwork.

There is only so much you can pack into a car and unless you have a large car and few belongings it will be stress full and a lot longer than you think.

Once you arrive in Spain the first problem is you are now on the other side of the road and things like parking barriers and entrances are all geared up for left hand drive cars. On main roads trying to get by that lorry or van will be difficult and dangerous as you can't see round them.

How long before it has to be registered?.

Under the EU directives you are considered to be a resident of Spain if you spend more than 183 days of the year here this is why you are only permitted to drive a UK Registered vehicle in Spain for up to six months of the year.

Beyond the six months you will need the following.

Register your UK vehicle in spain.
Drive or transport it back to the UK or at least out of Spain.
If you have moved to Spain with the intention of becoming a permanent resident here you must register your vehicle within 30 days with the local traffic department so if you own a property you have children in school owned a business or employed here you are registered.

Also you will need to make sure your car has an ITV thats the mot here in Spain.

This will mean getting the lights changed and having them go over the car with a fine tooth comb as they are now looking for a reason to get it off the roads here.

Once you have spent any amount of time in Spain you know the roadside checks by the police and Guardia Civil are an all too often occurrence.

Here the Spanish police can sometimes seem intimidating when it comes to checking your vehicle and documentation and if you are driving a foreign plated vehicle you will stand out like a sore thumb.

They know that most UK cars have not got all the right papers and they can make fines so that's why they love to stop UK cars here. If your car is registered and moted in the UK you can't get a UK mot here, it has to go through all the changes and paperwork and that is a lot of hassle trust me I have been there done that.

Also once your mot is out of date you can't drive it on the roads here and the police will fine you as your insurance is not invalid here. They will compound your car and it takes weeks to get sorted out.

What i did.

Don't start off with problems or possible problems it's the start of your dream so make it easy and enjoyable.

Hire a van or truck to bring it all here then fly over with a nice glass of wine on the plane and wait in a bar 2 days for it all to arrive and be unloaded for you, less stress and less effort.

Then go buy a Spanish car. You are going to live here now so be Spanish get a Spanish car. There's loads of good second hand cars here and local garages are full of cars that you can bargain on.

What I did was to go to a main dealer like one of the big car dealerships and ask them if they have any EX demo cars. These are cars that they have used for test drives and they are normally only 1 or 2 years old and the costs are a lot lower than new cars but you still get all the guarantees with them and buying from a main dealer you get better service and can always sell it back to them when you want to upgrade or change.

Where to buy a car.

A great site to search private sales is here.. https://www.milanuncios.com/coches-de-segunda-mano/

Just click the link above and type in the area you are in and the amount you want to buy and start searching. All private sales in Spain must come with a 6 month guarantee now.

 Also going to the local British community here there will always be someone who has or knows a guy selling a car here and at least you can speak to them in English if you're worried about buying from the Spanish.

Removals.

There are many UK companies doing daily removals to and from Spain, many do full or part loads at affordable rates and it's a lot less stress to get them to do all the hard work for you.

So search online to get a quote up front and remember that if you have bought an apartment here in Spain they sometimes need a lift system here to carry your furniture up the outside of the building.

This is a norm here but may cost you extra if it doesn't all fit in the sometimes small lifts here in Spain, so check first.

Remember also that there are Spanish companies going back to Spain that may do better deals as they are normally doing an empty return trip worth checking out.

Chapter 7
The Fastest Way To Learn Spanish

Learning Spanish is in my view ***the most important*** thing that you can do if you are ***moving to Spain*** and the number one reason most Brits fail here in the first few years is because they just don't bother or give up after a few months.

We Brits are slow when it comes to learning any languages and it's hard when most of the world speaks English now but Spain is a big place and many parts of Spain away from the touristy areas will not speak much English and most shops and businesses won't speak English at all.

Once you are living here you will need to speak Spanish or you will have to pay someone to help you with a variety of things like setting up bank accounts and direct debits for gas, water and light bills, plus translating all the letters you will start getting once you have a home here.

I remember when I was in school many years ago in the UK that we had 2 hours a week of French, well that's just not enough and I left school speaking no more than 5 or 6 words.

Here in Spain the kids start learning English at an early age and by the time they leave school most Spanish kids can speak 2 or 3 languages and many kids here speak very good English.

So what's best for you?

Well we all learn at different speeds and in different ways but below I will show you what I did and how I learned to speak pretty good Spanish in just a few months.

First off Lessons.

Well they say you should have lessons at a school or in a class but I just couldn't get on with it that way.

I remember the first few years when I was working for this English company here building and the son of the boss spoke very good Spanish, so none of us really had to but a few years later when I went self employed here I had to learn and learn fast...this is what I did.

I went to a local language school and arranged for private lessons 3 times a week and the first day we started writing out the verbs. After just 20 mins I asked the teacher how long till I could speak Spanish enough to order my materials and he said about 2 years. No No I said, this is not going to work for me I need to order materials this week.

He looked at me with bewilderment and shrugged his shoulders. I told him that I had an idea.

This is what I said to him " you be the shop owner and I will come in and ask for wood and things related to wood and you respond with words and phrases that I would hear and can use.

Role play was how I learned.

One day he would be the shop keeper of a glass shop the next a D.I.Y. shop then a paint shop and so on. I started to learn basic phrases for things that I would buy, need and use for work and just learned a few numbers and colors.

In just a few weeks I had enough words to get what I wanted and as the weeks went by we built on my vocabulary. Now I know this is not really the right way but it worked for me and I could speak basic Spanish in just a few weeks but it was limited to work and shops.

It takes years to learn all the complicated verbs past present and future and masculine and feminine and I am still learning them and getting them wrong but if you use the Spanish you know, often you start to pick up on others and it starts to sink in better than in a 1 hour class or at least that's what I feel.

My break up.

About this time I had split from my wife after 17 years of marriage as she wanted to go back to the UK and I did not, plus she missed her large family, so we ended up divorcing about 1 year later. We had a good marriage for 17 years but just grew apart and I think living here made her miss her family more, so we ended as friendly as possible for a divorce.

I found my weeks were mostly filled with my work or cleaning the house or walking my dog so I decided that I needed to get out and really start meeting new people and decided that I would concentrate on my Spanish but not in classes but face to face.

One day I saw a poster for a walking group day out in the hills, so found out where and when they met and went along to chat with them. Now this was not a British club it was all Spanish mostly youngish people and there was no English just me.

The guide told me that I could join but nobody spoke English except this one girl called Carmen who was about 26 and worked in a local office building near me.

So every other Sunday we would all meet up in some car park and head off on some new route in the hills one day and near the beach another. At the end of these walks that were about 3 to 4 hours, we would stop at a local bar or cafe to have a beer and snacks and this is where I really started to learn Spanish.

I would just start talking to people and they would talk back helping me with my poor Spanish and as the months went by my Spanish improved a lot.

One day after a long walk with the club one of the girls told me that they were going Salsa dancing that Saturday night at a bar in town that had free lessons.

They told me I should go as it was fun and I will meet new people to chat to.

At first I thought this was a very bad idea as the only dancing I did was when I was drunk at weddings. So after a bit I agreed to go and meet them that next Saturday night.

Well talk about a shock...

If you have ever seen the film "Dirty Dancing"?

well this was it but for real. It was a bar in the corner of a car park in town and as we went in there was salsa music playing and about 25 couples all dancing these complicated looking and very sexy dance moves. This was no dancing I had ever seen before and a bit of a shock. I felt very uncomfortable but told myself that nobody here knows me or really cares if I look a twit so just have a go.

Well after a few songs the music stopped and the classes begun and everyone had to pair up and as I started to look around for a partner this beautiful young girl grabbed my hand and pulled me into the middle of the class.

I had trouble following but each partner helped me and at the end of the 1 hour class I felt so relaxed and really enjoyed it even though I think I looked like a blind man walking through a mine field.

So weeks went by and I still went on the walks every other Sunday and now I was getting into the salsa dancing and going to 2 other bars so was now dancing 3 times a week. well why not I had nothing else to do in the evenings as I was living alone now.

My Spanish was getting pretty good now I thought and I started to date a few girls from the dance club and that really helps you speak Spanish.

OK so you may not want to go salsa dancing or walking but if you get out and join a club or just go where the Spanish go and chat face to face with them you will start to use the Spanish you know and improve upon it faster than in a 1 hour class writing out the verbs.

This really is the key.. using what you know even if its poor you will start to build on it and it's great to see the way a Spanish person talks face to face.

As I was learning Spanish at my lessons and at the clubs I also used a few apps and tapes in the car.

Now there are loads of great apps that you can download and many are free, I found that listening to them in the car as I was driving or on head phones when I was walking the dog was really helping.

Below are a few apps that i used and liked.

Learn online fast https://goo.gl/7pu4xL

FREE APPS.	Paid APPS
easy ten	Learm Phrases
Duolingo	Babbel upgrade
Babbel	buscu lear
Rosetta stone upgraded	Rosetta stone

Another thing that I did that really helps is watch TV and movies in Spanish with English subtitles or no subtitles at all just Spanish, now some John Wayne films sound funny in Spanish but it's a great way to see and hear Spanish all the time. Also the radio in the house and in the car put it on Spanish stations and it will start to sink in.

You are never too old to learn Spanish and if you really want to learn and you put in the effort you can learn fast and once you start to have a real chat with someone you will really appreciate it.

Personally its one of my pet hates here in Spain with the expats that don't bother to learn Spanish and these people are missing out on the real life here in Spain.

Like any new thing you learn, if you put in the time you get the rewards and we can make time, if you just think when you are doing something mundane you could be listening to a Spanish tape or app.

Where I use to live in Roquetas de mar there was also an English club that met up every Monday to chat and have a drink but these people didn't speak much Spanish even the ones that lived here a long time. These sort of English clubs are great when you first **move to Spain** as they can give you all the hot tips on where to get TV , trades people and where to go for the best tapas but I found that these places and the people get a bit boring after a few months as many of them don't really leave their tight little circles.

It's ok if you just want a mini England in Spain and a moan up about how you can't get your favorite tea bags but If you try and mix in with real Spanish people you will learn so much more and get to see the real side of how the Spanish live.

So now you know how to Learn Spanish fast....Download the apps get the tapes and practice what you learn even if it's only with your partner at home or online.

If you start with a new word a day then in a few months you will be able to speak a few phrases that will really help you once you are there.

CHAPTER 8
FINDING WORK IN SPAIN

So whether you need to earn a full time income in Spain or just enough to pay for your Tapas, finding work is what's on a lot of expats minds and one of the hardest things to do here in Spain for the English.

Yes you can get bar work or cleaning jobs here but these are very low paid jobs and the hours are long and the conditions not that great. Most of these jobs are back hand cash jobs that can get you and the employer in trouble.

 There are those who think it's great to do the airport runs. That's taking friends and people to the airport and picking them up again when they come back. This is illegal here and if caught by the police who are always at the airport you can have your car confiscated and fined plus your insurance will not cover you your car or them if you have an accident.

One other thing about these airport runs. I have seen on TV here that the taxis at the airport have caught on now and are on the lookout for this and they will damage you and your car if they see you doing this. so basically it's a no no.

Getting a full time job in Spain

Remember that Spain like many other countries has only just started to rise out of the big recession that hit here several years back. You will be competing with the local Spanish for jobs

Most big companies here are now only giving out 3 month contracts to all their workers as this way they pay less tax and can get rid of staff as and when they need to so finding a good job with a long term contract for more than 6 months is really hard here.

There's one other really important thing to remember as well

*DO YOU SPEAK SPANISH?...*If not then it's going to be even harder to find work here.

Last year I met an English guy in town who had just moved here with his wife and daughter, I asked him if he worked here and he said not yet but I will get a job soon. So I asked him what he was going to do?

He told me that he was going to get a job in a car rental place in tow, so I asked which one. He said " not sure yet I will have a look around in the next few weeks". ok I said so your Spanish is good then? "No" he said "I will just work for the British". I was shocked. ...really so what about if a Spanish person comes in and what about all the paper work that will have to be filled out that will all be in Spanish plus the phone calls will be in Spanish too. "O yes I hadn't thought of that" he said.

How I Found Work

I found work here when I first came here by going to British bars and just asking if anybody was looking for carpenters and I was very lucky that I found a guy who was building houses in the hills and needed workers he was also English and so was his customers but this was very lucky now I look back at it and it only lasted 2 years, then I went self employed as I wanted to go on my own and work where and when I wanted.

Going self-employed is a great idea for ex pats as most companies will take you on or offer you a few days' work here and there so you can get some experience with them and they can get to know you, plus you will find more work this way once you are out and about.

To get started as self-employed here you need to be registered at the tax office and have all the right papers and an accountant and pay you social security each month.

The social security I paid was about 300 a month and although this sounds a lot it does include all health cover for you and any other member of your close family wife and kids.

Even if you are not working here in Spain if you got registered as self-employed and paid your social each month you and your family will be covered for health if needed and that may be a lot cheaper than taking out private health cover for each of you.

Brexit is changing weekly so who knows what will happen or how long it will take to really sort it all out but Health cover here in Spain is a worry for Expats here so this could be a way around it.

A great way to find work here in Spain.

One thing I did when I was first self-employed and had a slow time was to go to local buildings and shops and factories where there was carpenters or any form of woodwork or building going on and ask them if I could work for them for FREE for a few weeks.

I told them I wanted work experience and would do anything for free for a while. Most times they had nothing but there was 2 occasions when I got work. Once I worked stacking sheets of ply in a ware house and after 2 days the owner saw me working well and asked if I could help another guy put some kitchen units together in the back of the factory.

After 3 days of this I was getting ready to pack it in then he offered me a job 3 days a week. This was really because he saw that I was a good worker and that I was already self-employed plus it fitted in great around the little work that I had of my own. I stayed here for about 2 months then I had a few good jobs that picked me up again.

Another time I did this was at a place that I found to buy my materials from. It was a timber yard and I worked for the owner on Saturday mornings for free loading lorries with wood. This lead to him getting me some work with another Spanish guy who was fitting kitchens but this time it was a paid job.

If you offer to work for free it sounds crazy but it's a great way of learning from them and making new contacts and it could lead to better things as it did for me.

If you have no work then it's better to work a few weeks for free on the chance of getting something else.

Doing a good CV In Spanish

A good CV here is also important and something else that works is this..

Do your CV in English and Spanish and then take it in person to places you think are looking or may be looking to hire.

Even if they are not try this..... Take your cv to say the shop you want to work in and tell them you are looking for a starter job and will consider anything but don't sound desperate just keep to work.

Then they will probably put it in the bottom drawer and forget about it and you but now after 3 days go back again don't call them go there in person and speak to the same person you handed it to and ask them what they thought.

Most times they probably never even read it but what the hell. Then if they say they haven't got anything ask them for feedback. Ask them what they thought you could do to make your cv better. They will nearly always give you some ideas and these are the things that they would be looking for so you can correct or adjust your cv to suit the next job prospect.

Online CV.

Put your cv online, like write a word document as you cv and then add a photo of you in the corner then jazz it up how you like but make it all fit on 1 page like a letter.

Then send this out in an email in Spanish to as many places as you can think of. Find online the name of the boss or company leader and send it to them my email there's always an email somewhere on websites.

Now send it as an attachment in the email and you will find that people nearly always open attachments in emails as they want to see what it is. This is a great way to get people to see and know about you and again follow it up a few days later with a visit or another email or call.

Once you have a 1 page email cv ready you can copy and paste it all day long to loads of perspective jobs.

This has worked for me a few times over the years here and can work for you, it just takes a little effort.

Chapter 9
Running A Business In Spain

So what's it like to run a business in Spain?

Well After the first few years working here I went self employed as a carpenter and builder so will tell you how it was for me and a few other Brits I worked with that had also started their own business here in Spain.

At first I was on my own and registered for tax and got myself a Spanish accountant that spoke Spanish because at that time my Spanish was still poor.

One great advantage of being self-employed is that once you are registered and start paying your monthly social security here (around 300 Euros a month) you and your immediate family wife and kids, will have access to the health cover here. As long as one member of the family pays the others are covered. This is a great way to get the whole family covered here even if you are not going to work as paying 300 a month may be cheaper than getting private health insurance for them all.

At the time of writing this book there are a lot of changes going on and with Brexit well who knows. I have heard that some places here are asking now for proof that the family all have private cover if you are living here and not working.

The main part of my work was at first working for expats here in Spain doing all sorts of odd jobs from basic maintenance to total kitchen refits and new bathrooms.

After a few years here my work was going well and I employed a guy called Steve to help me and decided to offer him a contract

This is a big deal here in Spain a contract job means he and his family get the benefits. So This was a hard working guy and I invited him and his wife to my house for dinner that night at 8.30 to sign contracts, My wife had prepared a meal for us all.

Then at 9pm I called him to ask where he was, He said that he was on his way and would be there in 10 mins. Not a good start as punctuality is a big thing for me.

At 9.45 they arrived and it was obvious that they had been drinking, I asked what happened and he said that they had watched the football match in the bar and it ran late. I tried to hide my anger and we had dinner and signed the contracts. I did have to force myself and thought then that it may be not such a good idea.

All was ok for about 3 weeks and then I had a trip to the UK to see my Parents and would only be away for 1 week.

There was a job that we had nearly finished and I told him that there was just the painting of the garden wall to do and then I could ask for full payment of the works.

I told Steve that if he could get the painting done in that time I would be happy and he could have the week off if finish early. There was about 3 to 4 days work but if he worked a little longer each day we agreed that he could get it done in 3 days and that I would pay him for the week.

On my return the first Monday morning at 7.30 my phone rang and it was the customer asking when we would finish the painting as he had not seen anyone there for 3 days.

That morning I ask Steve what was going on and he told me that he went there the first 2 days and then had friends come over from the UK so had to spend time with them and pick them up from the airport. I just couldn't believe what I was hearing as everyone here knows how valuable a full time contract job is.

I wanted to get rid of him there and then but it's not that easy with a contract so I asked my accountant what I needed to do.

He told me I needed to get him to sign a paper to say that he was leaving and that way I didn't have to pay him any extras.

The papers were all in Spanish and so I just told him that there was a few papers he forgot to sign and he just signed them. 2 days later I told him sorry Steve there's no more work and he left.

Another reason why you need to learn Spanish so you know what you are signing.

There was at this time 2 other guys from the UK who had also started their own business here, one was a metal worker fitting gates and doors to expats here and the other was a plumber working with his brother who could speak some Spanish.

First the Metal worker, well he had loads of work and was a very hard worker, working all hours to support his wife and kids. The only trouble was he liked to have a few beers at lunch and after work and this started to be a problem.

He did work for me many times as I would have customers who wanted things done and I measured up for new window grills or gates and this guy would make them and I would help him fit them and we shared the money. After a few years his drinking got too much for his wife and she told him "come back to UK with me or we split up now". Just 2 weeks later he was gone and today his old workshops stands empty here.

Spain has bars everywhere and with prices so cheap and no real closing times or opening times you can get a drink almost anywhere at any time.

Now the plumbers.

Well they had loads of work as well but when the crisis hit here it hit hard and one brother worked hard trying to drum up enough work and the other was just not that interested and as they were both taking a wage out of the business it just couldn't go on like that and they folding.

One brother returned to the UK and the other is still here doing well and just working on his own.

Many Brits come here and start up a business and think that it will be an easy life here but it's very hard especially at first and if you don't speak Spanish is even harder.

We are Going To Open A Bar

That's the words I heard one day as I was introduced to a new family from London that had just moved here. There was mum and dad, son and his girlfriend. Dad had sold a pub in London and they were going to open a bar on the beach and live the good life.

They wanted me to renovate the bar that they had just bought that week so I went along to take a look.

This was in a perfect area right in the corner of a very popular beach and had many people walking passed each day, all looked great from the outside.

It was a very small bar and they told me that they wanted it to be a sports bar for Brits and that they would take turns in running it, first week the mum and dad then the son and his girlfriend, not a bad idea really.

As I started to take measurements I saw that there was only 1 power point in the kitchen, now it was a small kitchen but only 1 power point was not going to work.

As we pulled out some of the old units we could not find any others so this was on the list of first things to do.

The quote was accepted and I put them in touch with my electrician who was coming on Monday to start the electrics.

First day of works and the electrician told me that the main fuse board would need to be updated as there was not enough power coming into the bar from the street. We had to call the power company to get them to ok it and they told us that the cable in the street was too small to upgrade the power and that they needed a stronger power input.

Price 8,000 Euros yes that's 8,000 because they needed a project license and a surveyor and architect to oversee the job plus council permission to dig up the street and it would take 3 weeks after they got permission that could take another month.

The power company man told me that the old owner had asked about this just 6 months ago and that's why they sold it and moved on. If only the new family had bothered to look in the kitchen a little better they may have seen this but I guess they were just very keen to buy the bar.

My Solution.

The family said that they had just bought 2 apartments near the bar to live in and a new car so could not pay that price.

My idea was to not do the works but to get all gas appliances, this was not ideal but a lot cheaper than paying 8,000 and we could still have all the works done and open in 2 weeks.

This is what they went for.

The bar opened and seemed to be going ok but they did not do Tapas in the bar and when you have loads of Spanish bars all in the same street and right next door that's a mistake.

They would charge a little more as their beers where mostly imported beers and although good beers with brand names here the Spanish like draft beer from the tap.

Several months went by and one day I was walking by and saw a new guy that was waiting on tables there and I knew him as he had lived here a few years and spoke Spanish well.

I asked what he was doing and he said that they were paying him to manage the bar and do all the ordering. The mum was in the kitchen and the rest of the family were on the beach nearby.

OK so now you have 4 people and a new waiter all taking wages from this small bar and trade going next door where the beer is cheaper and you get a free tapas included. Even a none bar person like me knows this cant last.

About 4 months later I walked passed the bar and it was completely closed up and shut up and a for sale sign up on the door.

IT CAN WORK IF YOU DO

There is one more example of running a business here that I would like to share.

They are a new couple who moved from the UK just a few years ago and bought a new house here and opened a barbers shop. Now they too had a dream of a better *life in Spain* and from almost day one they came crossed the reams of paper work and bureaucracy here and not speaking Spanish struggled at first.

Opening the shop had a different set of problems and they had to pay to get help but they didn't give up and even as people would pass by the shop saying that it wouldn't work in this area they pushed on.

One year later the shop is doing well and they both love it here and are very happy that they moved here.

The difference is they worked hard daily to get it done and what they didn't know how to do they got help with and They had to change their working hours to suit the Spanish times and this has put them in an even better position and have now got a great little business.

It's not easy starting a business in the UK and even harder here in Spain but it's like anything in life, you get out what you put in and now these 2 really are living a dream life here in Spain.

If you are thinking of starting or running a business here then there is a lot to research and get all the info before you commit to buying anything as Some Spanish agents and owners will see your eagerness and enthusiasm and may want to cash in on it.

Again here is where good sold research comes in and don't rush it.

If it doesn't feel right then it probably isn't.

CHAPTER 10
YOUR KIDS NEW LIFE IN SPAIN

Many expats who move or are thinking of *moving to Spain* are very worried about how their kids may fit in and adjust after taking them away from their UK school and friends.

Most kids will hate the idea at first and not want to start a new school in a new country with a new language but I have see it all before and it nearly always works out amazingly for all.

Example.

I know an English guy here who had a wife and little girl about 6 years old, they moved here and he worked making security grills but he only worked for Brits here and did not speak Spanish nor did any of his family but he still put his little girl in a new Spanish school here and the first few days she hated it.

Then she made a few new friends and being different here i.e. English in a Spanish school, the kids stick out a bit and will attract new friends a bit faster. Well this little girl had so many friends coming round to her house each day and her mum started to meet and befriend the mums too.

About 3 years later I had to go to this guys house to measure up for a new kitchen and as I was there in his kitchen his phone rang. He answered it and gave it straight to his now 9 year old daughter who spoke perfect Spanish.

It was a builders suppliers who wanted to say that his materials had arrived and that he could collect them that week.

His 9 year old daughter was relaying the message and translating perfectly for him so naturally it was amazing and made him feel a bit stupid.

At the weekends the kids are out with their new Spanish friends and they just seem to live more outdoors almost all day. As the weather here is great most of the year you will find them out rather than in doors watch tv or playing video games.

It really is a better way of life here for kids and after the initial upset of the move and new school they will love life here.

The guy I was talking about earlier stayed here another 3 years then his old boss offered him a job back in the north of England and the money was pretty good so he took it.

His daughter was so upset she didn't want to go back to the cold or another new school plus all her friends were Spanish now. I did speak on the phone to him several months after he moved back to the UK and he said he now thought it may have been a mistake as it was freezing cold there and the days always seem cloudy and miserable he missed the sun and way of life but that was it he had to make a go of it.

Still his daughter was now about 10 and could speak perfect Spanish and that was more than her new English school mates could I bet.

Kids adapt fast here and when it's possible to have a BBQ or go to the beach most weekends I think that helps and it is more family orientated here and you get more family time even if you work 5 days a week it's just the way the Spanish are.

Go into any Spanish bar or restaurants here and you will always see the families with all their kids even at the bar.

It's a great life here for kids, yours will love it here. Most of my friend's kids here that are English and in Spanish schools already speak 2 languages and learning a third, now back in the UK I think most kids struggle to speak one language correctly. But that's just me sounding like my old dad.

Really though the British kids here after they have settled in really do enjoy life more here and spend way more time outside rather than at the pc in their bedroom.

Chapter 11
Making Spanish friends

How easy is it and where do you start..

Above, Me and my new Spanish climbing Friends.

What are the Spanish people like?

Now I have a Spanish wife and am connected to her large family I think I can say what the Spanish people are really like and just how they live.

If you go to a bar here or you are out and about you will notice that Spanish people can be a little loud in the way they speak to each other. They are a very friendly people in general but sometimes slow at coming forward if you are new. Once you make the effort or take the first steps they open up fast and are very chatty.

Family is very important to the Spanish and they include the kids in everything. Most places in Spain still close up for siesta. That's normally around 2pm until 4.30pm. They pick up the kids from school at 2 and then whole family goes home for lunch ,this is normally a big deal and takes 1 to 2 hours. Then they normally return to work until 7 or 8 pm.

Dinner in the evening starts for most Spanish families at 9 or 10pm. This late hour is something that I found very hard to adapt to and still do. Going out in the evenings also is a late affair with most bars opening around 8.30 at night as most Spanish people go out about 9 or 10 at night to eat and drink.

I have been to a few Spanish weddings here and both started very late at night, something we Brits are not use to.

The last wedding was a cousin of my wife's in Granada and the wedding in the church started at 9pm. We then went to a hotel in Granada for the reception that started serving the first source at 11.45 at night. We finished the meal at 2am and then the dancing and music started and went on until 6 am, this is about the norm here in Spain for a wedding.

My brother comes here to visit us several times a year and he still finds it hard to get use to when we go out for tapas at 9.30pm as he says back in the UK that would be late.

Once you start to get accustomed to these later times you will find that the Spanish people normally like to meet up as we Brits do just to chat and have a drink but here when you buy a drink most parts of Spain have some sort of Tapas, that's a small plate of food that comes with the drink and is normally included in the price.

Here in Almeria the tapas are free and you can choose from a menu in most Spanish bars and these tapas are cooked fresh to order but other parts of Spain you may only get a small plate of crisps or olives and some bigger cities charge extra for the tapas so move to Almeria the food is FREE with a beer or wine.

Making new Spanish friends is easy if you just make the effort. Most older Spanish people will not speak any English even in the bigger cities but if you try your broken Spanish on them they will in most cases reply and try to help you.

In local villages like the one in the hills where my Spanish Wife is from, the people are more reserved and many have lived and worked in the same village all their life and many have never even been to the next major cities. That's why there are so many small villages closing down or has properties vacant due to the fact that the younger generation can't find work there or are wanting to travel away from village life so the population is slowly dyeing and these smaller villages are unfortunately going the same way.

Small village life is a lot different than the big towns and cities a very slower and quieter way of life in deed and if this appeals to you then do go there in the winter months because they are even quieter in winter as people don't venture out much at this time.

Village life and the fiestas are great and its really like being part of one big family but remember the whole village will get to know you and everything about you very fast. In some smaller villages and towns like my wife's even the police stations close at the weekends and there are no police anywhere.

If there is a major problem you need to call the national police but only in emergencies. Many of these also go very quiet for siestas and lunch for about 3 hours.

The one great thing about village life is the cost of living is really cheap and food and drinks are so much cheaper than even the nearest cities. Just last night my wife and I went into the village square here for drinks and tapas at the local bar, there's only 3 bars here. We had 2 beer and 2 wines and 4 plates of fresh cooked tapas and the total bill was 7.50 Euros for the lot. Now I bet back in the UK that would cost about that for 1 glass of wine on its own.

Last week we got invited to my wife's friend's house as there was a fiesta in the street there at the weekend and we would be having lunch at her house after we watch the procession go through the streets.

 A colorful loud affair with locals dressed in national costumes with woman in the famous colorful long Spanish dresses and even the very young girls are dress in national dress.

After we all went back to the friend's house and every one helped set the table on the outdoor terrace with seating for 20 people, this is about the normal amount of guests. Most woman had brought along a dish that they had made the night before and with the table set we all started to eat drink and chat.

The lunch started at about 3pm and at 8 pm we were still drinking local wine and small cakes that are normally follow the meal at fiestas.

It really is a great family orientated life style here and this happens almost monthly compared to the British birthday or Christmas family gatherings.

Making Spanish friends is easier if you are married to one but I also know many British people living here that have many Spanish friends and this is mostly because they put them self's out there and make that effort.

Once you have a Spanish friend they normally invite you to meet their other friends so the snow ball effect starts and before long you find yourself sitting amongst a group of loudly talking Spanish people all just enjoying the Spanish way of life and you to are now part of this community ...If you have made the effort.

A few weeks ago I visited my old home town here of Roquetas de mar where I used to live when I first moved to Spain. I saw a local British bar that's been here for years and saw from a distance a few people sitting there that I knew.

These bars are always popular with Expats and every main town has them but some people only ever go to the same few bars week in and week out. Ok everyone has a different way of life I know but it still shocks me that these people are missing out of the real part or Spain and if they just went to the Spanish bar a few doors down they may meet some real Spanish people and make some Spanish friends who could help them see a very different side of life in Spain.

I don't mean to down cry these bars as they can be a great way to meet people and get help and facts about the area from the local expats but years later I still see the same old Brits sitting in the same spot in the same bar chatting about the same old things and for me that's not why I moved here but each to their own I guess.

If you *move to Spain* and you really want to see and enjoy the Spanish way of life then you must make some effort and just go up to people and start to chat.

They will be friendly I promise and you may just make a great new Spanish friend who could help you experience a new way of life.

Expats meeting clubs in Almeria...
https://goo.gl/LFRVef

THERES LOADS MORE JUST GOOGLE THEM AND SEE WHATS IN YOUR AREA.

Chapter 12
Traveling Around Spain

In the 17 years I have lived here I have traveled around Spain a lot and since I married my Spanish wife **LLani** 7 years ago we have continued to travel even more as she works for the local government offices here in Almeria and her work often sends her on short trips around the country that I accompany her on to soak up these new cities.

So here is a list of just some of the Bigger places You may of heard of that I have now been to in Spain starting with my home town.

Almeria. Sevilla. Cordoba. Cadiz, Huelva, Barcelona. Madrid, Malaga, Granada, Guardix, Toledo, Zaragosa, Pamplona,

Alicante, Murcia, Marballa, Andora, Olite, Soria, Ciudad Real, T arrogona, Gerona, Figueras, Rosas, Gibralta, Torremolines, Jerez de la frontera.

Finana near Granada

There are many smaller villages and places along these routes that we have also visited.

People often say why are you going on holiday when you live in Spain or why do you travel so much.

Once you have lived here a few years it feels like home and like anyone else you like a holiday each year so we normally travel around Spain visiting my wife's family who are scattered all over Spain.

We also have a trip back to the UK to visit my old mum in my home town of Brighton southern England and I have taken my wife to Scotland a few times.

About 2 years ago now we did splash out and have 3 weeks traveling to our dream destination of Bora Bora and Tahiti and several of the islands in the south Pacific.

Now though with us about to start our latest adventure of building our dream home on a plot of land we have just bought here in Almeria, we only have my wife's shorter closer to home trips.

That's the great thing about living in Spain now, we are only a few hours' drive from some lovely famous Spanish cities that are full of amazing sights and sounds and Portugal another favorite place I holidayed when I was younger, is just 6 hours drive from where we now live.

So you see travel in Spain is easy and most of the roads are new and not that busy outside of Sevilla and Madrid. It's cheap to just get in your car and drive to them for the weekend to experience new places on a budget.

Week day accommodation in smaller hotels is the best way to do this we have found and booking a room online through a Spanish app or website will save you even more money.

There are a lot of new toll roads here now that you need to pay to use and some are a lot more than others and there is always a way around them even though maybe just a bit slower but some of these toll roads are worth taking like the one to Murcia that is about 12 euro's but when we used it we saw only 2 cars in over 1 hour of driving.

Normally when we travel here we take it in turns to drive for 2 hours each and then stop off at one of the hundreds of road site bars along the way for a quick coffee and bit to eat.

One of my hobbies is to collect knives and these road side bars always have a small glass cabinet somewhere inside near the bar that sell small pen knives or local workman's knives from around 10 euro's up to about 40 Euros.

Driving up to Sevilla a few months ago we passed many open field areas that had olive trees as far as the eye could see and the smell of the olives was very strong even with the windows closed. The same near Madrid with the rows and rows of Orange trees its quite a sight.

Not long ago we drove from Almeria up to my wife's sisters house in Pamplona, a drive of about 8 hours with several short stops along the way. Long motorways with light traffic all the way and not once did we see any traffic jams even when driving around Pamplona city.

Years ago when I lived in the UK I loved to go surfing down in Cornwall and drove there from Brighton about 6 hours but remember the roads would always be full of traffic and loads of caravans adding to the stress of the drive but nothing like that here in Spain.

David's Top 3 Cities you must see in Spain.

First off has to be Sevilla.

Full of history and amazing buildings to see like the Plaza de Espania with large open terrace and a big water fountain in the middle. The best way to see main attractions here is to just be a tourist and take the old fashioned horse and cart rides that you see offered in the main square and outside most main buildings.

They start at around 20 to 30 Euros and this includes the driver giving you a running commentary as you go. Ask for the park ride as some take you through the beautiful park on the way to the Plaza de Espania.

The cathedrals and churches are everywhere in Sevilla and worth a visit but remember in the summer months like July and August it gets very hot over 100 every day and there's no wind so it feels even hotter.

Along the river there are some great tapas bars and places to get a bite to eat. Evenings when the lights are all turned on the romantic atmosphere is amazing.

Places David has personally stayed in and would recommend are.

Hotels. ....Zenit, NH Collection, EX Sevilla Macarena, Eurostar Regina,

Use the Booking.com app and get €15 back with this coupon code: DAVIDI50 https://booking.com/s/73_4/davidi50

Make sure to go over the river to take a look round the old town of Trina is pretty there.

Second is Cordoba

Cordoba is really set around the famous Mezquita Catedral that dominates the city and is right in the center and this is where you want to stay but be warned parking is very difficult as the streets are very narrow but most hotels offer parking that can be pricey around 20 Euros a night but still worth it as parking outside and walking in is not a good idea.

Apart from visiting the amazing Mezquita you need to go to the Alcazar de los reyes Cristianos Gardens they are really beautiful.

If you get there before 10 you can sometimes get in for free for 1 hour. Use the front gate in the square to get in there is a guard there but he lets people in for 1 hour before it is open to public.

The Mezquita

Also there are the famous Spanish dancing horses that are just 10 mins from the Mezquita, there are shows most nights in the outdoor or indoor arena and what these amazing horses can do is truly astonishing.

This is a must for all the family and the show lasts about 1 hour and then you can see the stables after. Get there early or book at gate or online the day before or seats will be at the back.

The patios are also famous and all within walking distance of the center. These patios are normally open in May and some are free to enter some there is a small charge and tickets are on sale most places.

These patios are private houses that the people open to the public and they are full of amazing flowers that they attend to all year and then enter the patio into a competition at the end.

Make time to visit amazing Patios of Cordoba

The patios website is here, best deal is to book at little office in street near the patios just ask a local they know where it is...
https://woowcordoba.es/tour/patios-del-alcazar-viejo/

Places David has personally stayed in and would recommend are.

Hotels.   Eurostars Conquistador, Eurostars maimonides

These 2 hotels are right in front of the Mezquita and very nice 4 star there are hostels in the area that are a lot cheaper but I normally book online 3 days before to get the best prices. Don't have breakfast its better and cheaper to eat in the street cafes.

The third place is Almeria

Now this is not just because I have lived here for 17 years but after traveling a lot around Spain I find this city has everything or that I can travel to in just a short car ride.

Example.

At the moment i am living in Retamar just outside the main town of Almeria but have lived right in the center and surrounding areas so know it very well. The clean sandy beaches are famous here and they just filmed the last Terminator film here in Almeria on the beach.

Also there are many other famous films that have been made here like A fist full of dollars, a few dollars more , the good the bad and the ugly. Conan the Barbarian' and even Indiana Jones and the Last crusade.

There is a Famous working film studio in the desert here that you can visit. Then just 2 hours drive up the road there is the ski resort of the sierra Nevada where you can ski from November to march and all for around 80 Euros including all passes and clothing hire.

I personally have skied here many times and many days in just a T shirt as the sun is warm and strong.

You can book online here..
https://sierranevada.es/

Then you have nearby the largest mountain in Spain

Mulhacen at almost 12,000 feet. And yes i have climbed it all the way to the top with my Spanish climbing club several years ago, it took 2 days and the view was incredible.

FREE Tapas.

Yes Almeria is famous for FREE Tapas, that's small plates of food normally grilled chicken, pork or beef and fish dishes.

You can get Tapas all over Spain but only in Almeria are they free to order from a menu and cooked fresh to order. Other parts of Spain you will get what the owner gives you or you can pay extra for a tapas.

Almeria s tapas are free with a beer or wine if you order a soft drink you can still have a tapa but you pay for it.

The cost of a beer in Almeria is around 2.euros to 2.50 with a free tapa. A glass of wine about 1.80.

In smaller villages like my wife's village of Finana we pay 1.20 a beer and 1.30 a wine with a free tapa. ...The history of the Spanish tapas here... https://goo.gl/JaAm83

Yes many areas do have tapas but in most places outside of Almeria you don't get to choose off a menu and cooked fresh to order. Anothetr great reason to try out Almeria.

Almeria has an international airport and daily flights to many top airports in the uk.

Places to Stay.

In Roquetas de mar a very popular tourist area there are all nationalities and loads of bars and shops with great wide sandy beaches and all year round sun even in December you can sunbath on the beach .

There are many hotels along the front there and loads of places to rent from small apartments up to villas with pools.

For best prices book online also I recommend these local agents that I know and have used for clients and friends. Here is their websites. or try "On The Beach com

More info on Almeria here...

https://goo.gl/h6PdEe

https://goo.gl/ui8W8h

https://goo.gl/d3q5HJ

There are many lovely places to visit in Spain once you are here and there is something to suit all tastes so just get in your car and go for a ride you may find a gem.

Some of the best apps and sites we use for travel.

Use the Booking.com app and get €15 back with this coupon code: DAVIDI50 https://booking.com/s/73_4/davidi50

Booking com   Trip advisor   Trivargo Minanuncios.   Zenit

Our Blog Here https://britishexpatsinspain.com/

Podcast show

https://www.spreaker.com/show/living-in-spain-with-david-wright

My new podcast show has new podcast episodes uploaded with new guests every week.

This is the end of this book but can be just the start to your New Adventure in Spain.

I interview expats here with businesses and families that have done what you want to do and living as you want in amazing places all over Spain so come have a listen as you will learn some amazing free tips and advice from them.

CHAPTER 13

Living in Spain after Brexit

Yes ok so there have been some changes and some new rules and requirements to live in Spain now but there are still people moving here even now with Brexit in place and the virus.

!8 years ago when I first moved to Spain there were loads of things that I didn't know or understand and there were papers and documents that I had no idea of how to get. You know what ? I did it anyway.

The point is there will always be reasons and obstacles trying to stop you following your dreams and its only with hard work and persistence that you can get past these.

It's never going to be the right time and theres always going to be reasons that YOU think are stopping you BUT if you really want it and you take action then anything is possible.

My personal opinion is that we have all had 4 years to prepare for Brexit and some say that they were not in a position to do it back then. Well 4 years is long enough to make new plans to get where you want. OK I know not everyone can do it and some people are only just now wanting to Move to Spain. The thing is they still can

You just need to think of ways that you can meet the new requirements.

Many say it's the money. But there is a lot you can do to get that money if that's all that's stopping you from following your dreams. Maybe a new job or 2 jobs or re train to learn more skills and make yourself more valuable. Just how much do you want it?

The virus and Brexit have made it harder to move to Spain and living here is more difficult but it is so in most countries at the moment so just thing where would you rather be.

Look the most important thing is time and health. We have so little time really and our health declines every week so you owe it to yourself to live the life you want now before its too late. So many times when I was young at my first jobs did I see old boys telling us young lads what a lovely time they were going to have out playing golf all day or just doing nothing once they retired.

I personally know several of these old boys that never even made it to retirement they died off just a few years before so all those years paying into the pensions and saving was for what?

Yes we need to plan for older age but we also need to live life to the full now as we don't know whats round the corner.

When people ask me when the best time to move to Spain I always is say NOW.

Right now as I write this I am looking out of my home office window in the house that I built with my wife and the sun is out and there's no clouds in the sky just strong blue sky and I know manana will be pretty much the same.

I loved my home town of Brighton and like to visit there every few years but I just don't want to live there any more or follow that rat race style of life.

Even with the restriction's here, that will lift in time its still better to be here in the sun and enjoy the Spanish way of life. Maybe I am biased after 18 years here but I have been to over 20 different countries around the world and still think this is the best place to live.

If you would like to see Davids BBC TV interview or his pod casts or Radio interviews then they are all free on his log here www.britisexpatsinspain.com

I hope this book has been helpful in giving you an idea of what it's like and what you need to do if you are thinking of MOVING TO SPAIN

Please come over to our FaceBook group and tell us what you think

Find us on FaceBook Groups.... "British Expats In Spain"

Watch all my videos on my YouTube channel here www.youtube.com/c/DavidWrightBritishExpatsInSpain

Remember to go and check out my new book in this series that's called **"Finding Work In Spain"**

Is on Amazon and it's a free download on Kindle for some devices.

...THE END...

Of this book

but the start of your dream. Now go make it happen.

Remember to leave a nice review on Amazon and you will be automatically added to the party list at my new house this year.